THE G.I. SERIES

The United States Marine Corps

First Lieutenant Thomas English, about 1826. In 1821, Marine lieutenants gave up the double-breasted coat and tight fitting breeches in favour of single-breasted coatees and loose Cossack-style trousers. The heavily laced coats featured the newly fashionable Prussian-style standing collars and carried wings rather than epaulets. All lace ended in the distinctive diamond or 'bastion' points. Since the use of wings made the old depiction of rank with the epaulet impossible, specific rank was indicated by gold chevrons, worn on the sleeves points down. Second lieutenants had a single chevron on the right sleeve and first lieutenants had a chevron on each sleeve. Lieutenant English's uniform conforms to the regulations except his chevrons are placed points up. This portrait is the earliest known depiction of the Marine Mameluke sword. In the autumn of 1825, the Quartermaster Department purchased enough Mameluke swords of this pattern from England and it received and distributed the swords a few months later to all officers. Several swords from this consignment survive and they are of a uniform pattern, similar to the modern Marine sword but with an all-brass scabbard. The first pattern Mameluke sword remained in use until 1859. (Photograph courtesy of the National Park Service, Springfield Armory.)

THE G.I. SERIES

THE ILLUSTRATED HISTORY OF THE AMERICAN SOLDIER, HIS UNIFORM AND HIS EQUIPMENT

The United States Marine Corps

Charles H. Cureton

Greenhill Books
LONDON

Stackpole Books
PENNSYLVANIA

Greenhill Books

The United States Marine Corps first published 1997 by Greenhill Books, Lionel Leventhal Limited, Park House, 1 Russell Gardens, London NW11 9NN
and
Stackpole Books, 5067 Ritter Road, Mechanicsburg, PA 17055, USA

British Library Cataloguing in Publication Data
Cureton, Charles H.
The United States Marine Corps. - (G. I. Series: the illustrated history of the American Soldier, his uniform and his equipment; 9)
1. United States. Marine Corps – Uniforms – History
I. Title
359.9'6'14'0973

ISBN 1-85367-289-0

Library of Congress Cataloging-in-Publication Data
Cureton, Charles H.
The United States Marine Corps/by Charles H. Cureton. 72p. 26cm – (G.I. The illustrated history of the American soldier, his uniform and his equipment: 9)
ISBN 1-85367-289-0 (pb)
1. United States. Marine Corps. I. Title. II. Series: G. I. Series: 9.
VE23.C87 1997
359.9'6'0973–dc21

DEDICATION
To my wife Caroline, for her assistance with the manuscript.

ACKNOWLEDGEMENTS
I would like to acknowledge the help and assistance provided by the Marine Corps Historical Center and Museum, particularly Mr Ken Smith-Christmas and Ms Lena Kaljot.

Designed and edited by DAG Publications Ltd
Designed by David Gibbons
Layout by Anthony A. Evans
Printed in Hong Kong.

THE UNITED STATES MARINE CORPS

The United States Marine Corps was first created when, on 10 November 1775, Continental Congress passed a resolution to raise 'two Battalions of Marines' for service as landing forces for the Navy. Serving on land and at sea, the Continental Marines distinguished themselves in a number of operations including their first amphibious raid into the Bahamas in March 1776, under the command of Captain Samuel Nicholas. Nicholas was later promoted to major and, as the senior officer of Marines during the Revolutionary War, is considered the first Marine Commandant. The Treaty of Paris, April 1783, concluded the Revolutionary War and as the last of the Navy's ships were sold, the Continental Navy and Marines went out of existence.

Tensions between the United States and France led to the formal re-establishment of the Marine Corps on 11 July 1798, although some ships' detachments had actually been organized the year before. The legislation of July 1798 established the authority for these units and created the basic organization and command structure from which the future Marine Corps was to emerge. Marine ships' detachments saw action in the quasi-war with France (1798–1800), landed in Santo Domingo (1800) and took part in operations against the Barbary pirates along the 'Shores of Tripoli' (1801–15).

During the War of 1812, sea-going detachments participated in naval operations and land-based units participated in the defence of Washington D.C., at Bladensburg, Maryland (1814), and joined with Andrew Jackson's forces in defeating the British attack on New Orleans (1815). In the decades following the war, Marine ships' detachments protected American interests around the world including the Caribbean (1821–22), the Falkland Islands (1832), Sumatra (1831–32), off the coast of West Africa (1820–61) and in the operations against the Seminole Indians in Florida (1836–42).

During the Mexican War (1846–48), Marines seized enemy seaports on both the Gulf and Pacific coasts. In addition, a battalion of Marines joined General Scott's army and participated in the American campaign that captured Mexico City, the 'Halls of Montezuma'.

Marines served ashore and afloat in the American Civil War (1861–1865). Although most service was on ships, a battalion fought at Bull Run in 1861, and other units saw frequent action, conducting raids and forming landing parties, with the blockading squadrons at such places as Cape Hatteras, New Orleans, Charleston and Fort Fisher. In the last decades of the nineteenth century, Marines made numerous landings throughout the world, especially in the Orient and in the Caribbean area.

Following the Spanish–American War (1898), in which Marines performed with valour in Cuba, Puerto Rico, Guam, and the Philippines, the Corps entered an era of expansion and professional development. Marine battalions saw active service in the Philippine Insurrection (1899–1902), the

Boxer Rebellion in China (1900), Nicaragua (1899, 1909-10, 1912-13), Panama (1901, 1902, 1903-04), the Dominican Republic (1903-04, 1916-24), Cuba (1906-09, 1912, 1917), Mexico (1914) and Haiti (1915-34).

World War I defined the Marine Corps for the American public in a way that had not been done before. Aviation and ground units distinguished themselves on the battlefields of France (with the 4th Marine Brigade earning the title of 'Devil Dogs' for the heroic action at Belleau Wood). Marine aviation, which dates from the training of First Lieutenant Alfred A. Cunningham in the summer of 1912, flew day bomber missions over France and Belgium. More than 30,000 Marines served in France; over one third were killed or wounded in six months of intense fighting.

Prior to World War II, the Marine Corps began to develop the doctrine, equipment, and organization needed for amphibious warfare. The success of this effort was evident at Guadalcanal in 1942, and later at Bougainville, Tarawa, New Britain, Kwajalein, Eniwetok, Saipan, Guam, Tinian, Peleliu, Iwo Jima and Okinawa. By 1945, the Marine Corps had grown to include six divisions, five air wings and supporting troops, making a total of 485,113 men and women. The war cost the Marines nearly 87,000 dead and wounded, with 81 Marines earning the Medal of Honor.

Landing at Inchon, Korea, in September 1950, Marines achieved a dramatic victory that pushed the North Korean Army out of South Korea and proved that the doctrine of amphibious assault was still viable. After the recapture of Seoul, the Marines advanced to the Chosin Reservoir, only to find that the Chinese had entered the war. After years of offensives, counter-offensives, seemingly endless trench warfare and occupation duty, the last Marine ground troops were withdrawn in March 1955. More than 25,000 Marines had been killed or wounded during the Korean War.

The Marine Corps was actively engaged in the years following the conflict in Korea. In July 1958, a brigade-sized force landed in Lebanon to restore order. During the Cuban Missile Crisis, in October 1962, a large amphibious force was mobilized but not landed. In April 1965, a brigade of Marines landed in the Dominican Republic to protect Americans and evacuate those who wished to leave.

The landing of the 9th Marine Expeditionary Brigade at Da Nang in 1965 marked the beginning of largescale Marine involvement in Vietnam. By the summer of 1968, after the North Vietnamese Tet Offensive, Marine Corps strength in Vietnam rose to a peak of approximately 85,000. The Marine withdrawal began in 1969 as the South Vietnamese began to assume a larger role in the fighting, and the last ground forces were withdrawn by June 1971. The Vietnam War, the longest in the history of the Marine Corps, exacted a high cost with over 13,000 Marines being killed and more than 88,000 wounded.

In July 1974, Marines aided in the evacuation of American citizens and foreign nationals during unrest in Cyprus. The following year the collapse of South Vietnam led to Marine forces evacuating embassy staffs, American citizens, and refugees from Pnomh Penh, Cambodia, and Saigon. Later, in May 1975, Marines played an integral role in the rescue of the crew of the SS *Mayaguez* captured off the coast of Cambodia.

The mid-1970s saw the Marine Corps assume an increasingly significant role in defending the North Atlantic Treaty Organization's northern flank. Amphibious units of the 2nd Marine Division participated in exercises throughout northern Europe. The Marine Corps also had a key role in the development of the Rapid Deployment Force, a multi-service organization created to ensure a flexible military response around the world when needed. The Maritime Prepositioning Ships (MPS) concept was developed to enhance this capability by prestaging equipment to the designated area of operations, while Marine forces travelled by air to link up with the equipment.

The 1980s were characterized by an increasing number of terrorist attacks on United States embassies around the world. Marine Security Guards, under the direction of the State Department, were involved in defending these embassies. In August 1982, Marine amphibious units landed at Beirut, Lebanon, as part of the multi-national peace keeping force. For nineteen months these units were continuously engaged in keeping the warring factions apart. American ground forces were ultimately withdrawn following the terrorist bombing of the Marine barracks. In October 1983, Marine units were also part of the successful intervention in Grenada.

As the 1980s came to a close, Marine forces were deployed in response to instability in Central America. Operation JUST CAUSE, in December 1989, saw intervention in Panama to restore democracy. Yet, that event was overshadowed within a year when, in August 1990, Iraq invaded Kuwait and this set in motion the creation of one of the largest multi-national forces since the Korean War, and the largest deployment of Marine Corps forces in four decades. Between August 1990 and January 1991, 24 infantry battalions, 40 air squadrons, and the majority of the support units, totalling more than 92,000 Marines arrived in the Persian Gulf as part of Operation DESERT SHIELD. Operation DESERT STORM, the air and ground offensive, began on 16 January 1991 with air attacks against Iraqi positions. The ground campaign began on 24 February when the 1st and 2nd Marine Divisions broke through the Iraqi lines, along the Kuwaiti border with Saudi Arabia, and drove into occupied Kuwait. At sea, two Marine Expeditionary Brigades posed an amphibious threat to the Iraqi left flank and successfully tied up some 50,000 troops along the coast. By the morning of 28 February most of the Iraqi Army in Kuwait had been encircled.

In December 1992, Marine units landed in Somalia and began a two-year humanitarian relief operation in that strife-torn country. Further north, in Europe, Marine Corps air units joined in the effort to enforce a no-fly zone over Bosnia-Herzegovina. When civil unrest occurred in Rwanda in April 1994, Marine forces helped evacuate American citizens from that country. Marines also went ashore in September 1994 to help restore democracy in Haiti.

The history of Marine Corps' dress is as much about continuity as it is about change. The modern enlisted dress uniform is the direct descendant from the enlisted undress uniform established in 1859 and the Marine Corps' eagle-and-anchor buttons are scarcely altered from the pattern adopted in about 1804. As for officer clothing, the dress uniform is little different from that first prescribed in 1904 as undress, and the current evening dress uniform has its origins in the officers' fatigue jackets introduced in the 1839 uniform changes. The Mameluke sword was adopted in 1826, the quatrefoil on the top of officers' caps came into use in 1859, and the red stripe first appeared in 1849. The current service dress uniform is almost identical to the pattern described in the 1926 regulations. These are but a few examples.

Like all military clothing, Marine uniforms have evolved over the years, even if sometimes only in subtle ways such as an added waist seam or the introduction of synthetic fabrics, within the context of civilian fashion, cultural change and institutional requirements. They have changed in dramatic ways too, including the move from fitted narrow skirted coats to the loose fitting frock coats of the 1859 regulations. The introduction of khaki service dress at the turn of the century was equally dramatic, as was the adoption of the sage green utility dress as a combat uniform in 1942. Further dramatic departures include the development of jungle camouflage utilities in the late 1970s and the adoption of the Kevlar helmet in the 1980s. Yet Marine Corps dress has the unifying thread of being immediately identifiable. It inspired and continues to engender an especially strong sense of identity, loyalty and comradeship.

Uniform has always been central to maintaining the discipline deemed essential for the Marine Corps in its early role as a shipboard security force and ground attack element. From the day of a recruit's enlistment, maintaining the uniform to the high standards expected required constant attention and work. Upkeep of dress, equipment and weapons, served to reinforce drill and training to produce a Marine Corps noted for its discipline. This is of course true for many military organizations throughout history, but the Marine Corps cultivated its symbols and maintained a continuity in its dress that surpassed other American military organizations. The uniform moulded individuals as much as it defined them.

Marine dress has always underscored rank and authority. The status of non-commissioned officers over the rank and file, and the position of commissioned officers in relation to enlisted Marines, has always been clearly defined and given emphasis in almost every uniform adopted. Even in the modern combat uniform, Marine dress defines four basic groups, three of which are central to the hierarchical structure. The three rank groups are officers, non-commissioned officers and privates. Musicians made up a fourth group but, as communicators, they were not part of the command structure. The uniform further defined the significant gradations that existed with the ranks of commissioned and non-commissioned officers. By the twentieth century, the officer ranks were made up of general officers, field grade officers, and company grade officers. Non-commissioned officer grades have fluctuated somewhat but not in the distinction between staff non-commissioned officers and all other non-commissioned officers. These four groups were identified by differences in the design of their dress and the use of embellishments that were unique to a particular group. These differences are taught to every Marine during their initial training.

Over time, myths have developed over the origins of such items of dress as the Mameluke sword, the red stripe on the trousers and the quatrefoil on officers' caps. The importance of factual accounts is overshadowed by the effect of these stories on the imagination and the way they help recruits identify with the Corps' heritage.

The images presented in this book span the history of the Marine Corps since its establishment in 1798 and demonstrate the constancy of the image and the heritage of this elite formation. Undoubtedly, its uniform will continue to evolve as the Marine Corps meets the challenges of the next century and history shows that it will do so within the framework of tradition and its long-standing symbols.

FOR FURTHER READING

Cureton, Charles H. *U.S. Marines in the Persian Gulf, 1990–91: With the First Marine Division in Desert Shield and Desert Storm*. Washington, Marine Corps History and Museums Division, 1993.

Driscoll, John A. *The Eagle, Globe and Anchor*. Washington, Marine Corps History and Museums Division, 1977.

McClellan, Edwin North. *Uniforms of the American Marines: 1775–1829*. Washington, Marine Corps History and Museums Division, 1982.

Moran, Jim. *U.S. Marine Corps Uniforms and Equipment in World War II*. London, Winrow and Greene, 1993.

Stanton, Shelby. *U.S. Army Uniforms of the Korean War*. Mechanicsburg, Stackpole Books, 1992.

Stanton, Shelby. *U.S. Army Uniforms of the Vietnam War*. Mechanicsburg, Stackpole Books, 1989.

First Lieutenant Charles Broom, c.1813. The two-piece belt-plate was replaced in about 1812 by the gilt single-piece oval plate shown here. At least two of these plates survive to the present and, though differing in minor details, both were engraved with an eagle grasping an anchor. Marine officers' sashes were scarlet silk net.

Above: Orderly sergeant in summer dress, 1827, painted by Private E. C. Young, USMC. In 1827, Private E. C. Young painted this watercolour of the orderly sergeant who commanded his detachment. The painting accurately depicted the enlisted uniform in general use by that year, as well as showing a number of details unique to Marine non-commissioned officers. Orderly sergeants were sergeants in command of small ships' detachments and, as a mark of their position, they wore scarlet wool sashes in addition to the non-commissioned officers' sword. Lesser ranking sergeants also carried this sword but were equipped with muskets and related accoutrements in addition. The eagle-headed sword shown in the painting was regulations from the mid-1820s until 1859. Chevrons depicting non-commissioned officer grades were prescribed on 29 June 1822. They were to be of yellow lace and senior non-commissioned officers were to be distinguished by two chevrons on the right arm above the elbow. Private Young shows three chevrons on the right arm and each stripe was looped back on itself in the British style and set on a scarlet base. It is possible that orderly sergeants

who ranked above other sergeants were allowed the additional chevron. After 1827, the eagle on the breast and waist-belt plates was dispensed with. Marine muskets were not equipped with slings until the 1859 uniform and equipment changes.

Above right: Second Lieutenant Addison Garland, 1835. In 1834, President Andrew Jackson recommended to Commandant of the Marine Corps, Archibald Henderson, that an Army-style uniform be adopted. The Marine version was green in colour and edged in buff (actually an off-white) with buff turnbacks, and gray trousers trimmed on the outside seam with a 1½ inch wide buff stripe. The white leather waist belt had a Navy eagle-and-anchor belt-plate and the sword was suspended from a sliding frog. Lieutenant Garland has the chapeau authorized for all officers during the period 1834–35. After 1835, the chapeau was reserved for staff and field grade officers.

Right: Commandant of the Marine Corps Archibald Henderson, about 1847. This colour tinted image of Commandant Henderson shows the slashed cuff, stipulated for field grade officers, with lace similar to the pattern seen on other Marine officer coats of the period. As the uniform of the commandant, Archibald Henderson's dress has two features distinctive of his position. The epaulets featured the silver star of a brigadier general, a rank Henderson held by virtue of brevet promotion and as the authorized rank device granted by the Navy Department to the position Commandant of Marines. The second distinctive feature was the 1¾ inch wide gold trouser stripe; all other officers wore dark blue edged red stripes, 1839–49, and, after 1849, red stripes. The epaulets and gold trouser stripes are the earliest known use of unique devices to distinguish the commandant from other Marine officers.

Below: Enlisted Marines in dress and undress as illustrated in the 1859 regulations. The 1859 uniform continued the epaulets and the collar and cuff lace of the previous uniform but added the Army-style chevron system of 1847. A significant change also occurred in accoutrements with the decision to shift the cartridge box and the bayonet scabbard from shoulder belts to the waist belt. Marine accoutrement belts were white in contrast to Army belts which had been black since 1851. A French-style cap came into use and its front plate substituted the bugle-horn for the previous eagle-and-anchor device. Of these changes, the placement of accoutrements directly on the waist belt proved unpopular and the Quartermaster Department never fully implemented it. There were, however, two significant and lasting developments in enlisted dress with the 1859 changes. The single-breasted undress coat shown on the right was the forerunner of the current enlisted dress coat, and non-commissioned officers received a modified version of the Army-style foot officer sword. This sword is still in use today by Marine non-commissioned officers.

Above left: John Philip Sousa, Leader of the Marine Corps Band, about 1890, painted by Lieutenant Colonel J. J. Capolino, USMC. The present bandmaster's uniform is based on this design introduced in May 1875. Sousa's dress coat combined the lace arrangement used on the front of contemporary British hussar coats with the traditional red worn by Marine musicians to produce a uniform which has endured, with only minor changes, for over a century. As with his predecessors since 1834, Sousa's uniform included second lieutenant's epaulets, gold cord and lace, and an aiguillette. The red and white plume was adopted by the Marine Corps Band during the 1850s and was not used by musicians assigned to barrack guards or ships' detachments.

Above: Sergeants, ship's detachment, dress, about 1940. The sleeve of the sergeant on the right was twisted to show the star and gun sight device, signifying gun pointer first class.

Left: Male and female officers, summer service dress, 1972. Summer service uniform was worn prior to being phased out in the late 1970s and replaced by the all-season green uniform.

Tracked vehicle crewman, Saudi Arabia, January 1991, painting by Lieutenant Colonel Donna Neary, USMCR. Tank and Assault Amphibian Vehicle crews wore special Nomex fire-resistant overalls of an olive green colour. Special close-fitting armour protective vests and CVC helmets complete this uniform. During the Gulf War, the threat of chemical and biological weapons led to American servicemen and women wearing the gas mask in its carrying case at all times. The prescribed placement of the gas mask case was on the left leg as shown in the painting. When the ground offensive began in February, green camouflage chemical protective suits were worn over this uniform. The goggles and improvised face cloth were essential as protection against sand and dust.

Left: Gun crew, desert camouflage utilities, Saudi–Kuwait border, 20 February 1991. Artillery raids consisted of rapidly deployed artillery units operating by day and night. Camouflage netting was not used due to the short duration of these actions. Chemical protective suits were not worn on the raids. (Photograph courtesy of Combat Camera, 1st Marine Division.)

Bottom left: Captain John Allison, Chemical Protective Suit and flak vest, 1st Marine Division, Kuwait, 26 February 1991. The threat of Iraqi chemical and biological weapons caused American forces to wear specially designed charcoal-lined protective suits. Thus attired, distinctive insignia disappeared from view and it was only possible to determine one organization from another by small details. The policy in the 1st Marine Division was to wear the flak jacket over the chemical protective suit while for the 2nd Marine Division it was the other way round. Captain Allison has on the communications helmet and goggles issued to personnel operating tracked vehicles. This photograph was taken in the middle of the burning oil fields and Captain Allison's face shows the grime produced by oil droplets in the air. Note the tip of the plastic spoon used for eating field rations.

Right: Helicopter pilot, flight clothing and equipment, Saudi Arabia, January 1991. The Nomex clothing and harness with flight equipment for helicopter pilots and crews were now rigidly standardized. Some desert-coloured flight clothing and helmet covers were provided during the Gulf War, but many continued to wear green clothing.

Above: Non-commissioned officers, 1st Marine Division, desert battle dress uniform, Saudi Arabia, late November 1990. The three non-com missioned officers awaiting President George Bush's visit to the 1st Marine Division on Thanksgiving Day, display the typical dress and equipment of Marines in the desert. The desert battle dress uniform (DBDU) hat is shown being worn in the prescribed manner without a rolled, shaped or stiffened brim.

Left: Enlisted man, 1st Marine Division, desert batle dress uniform, Saudi Arabia, December 1990. Deser camouflage covers for flak jackets were not available in sufficient quan tities for every Marine deployed in Saudi Arabia, and particularly those arriving in January 1991.

Left: First Lieutenant Daniel Sutherland, about 1847. This image shows the future Quartermaster of the Marine Corps at the time of his promotion to first lieutenant in 1847. He was dressed in the officers' regulation 1839 full dress uniform as prescribed for lieutenants. The coat was dark blue, faced red, with gold vellum lace to collar, slashed cuffs and skirts. Coats of the period were padded in the chest and fitted to the body and arms. The trousers were light blue with 1½ inch wide dark blue stripes edged in red (total width was 1¾ inches) and placed along the front edge of the outer seams. Lieutenant Sutherland's rank can be deduced by a narrow bullion fringe on the epaulets and the two loops (just visible on his left sleeve) on the cuffs. This is one of the few extant photographs showing the dress belt with its sliding frog for the Mameluke sword. (Photograph from the Dr. William Schultz collection.)

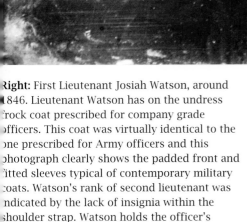

Right: First Lieutenant Josiah Watson, around 1846. Lieutenant Watson has on the undress frock coat prescribed for company grade officers. This coat was virtually identical to the one prescribed for Army officers and this photograph clearly shows the padded front and fitted sleeves typical of contemporary military coats. Watson's rank of second lieutenant was indicated by the lack of insignia within the shoulder strap. Watson holds the officer's fatigue cap with the prescribed gold embroidered wreath-and-anchor device. Enlisted fatigue caps had 'USM' in block letters instead. Photograph courtesy of the Dr. William Schultz collection.)

Left: Unidentified corporal, around 1852. In viewing nineteenth century images, it is necessary to remember that yellow photographed dark, making yellow lace difficult to see against dark backgrounds as in this studio portrait. There are a number of intriguing details in this image. The army-style all wool epaulets had changed to epaulets of yellow wool straps with brass crescents. The narrow bullion fringe, in combination with two loops to the cuff, establishes the sitter as a corporal as a private would not have had any fringe. His black leather stock, seen between the collar and neck, makes this one of the few images to show why Marines were called 'Leathernecks'. The bell crown uniform cap and eagle-and-anchor device were the patterns adopted in 1846; however, the plain brass oval shoulder and rectangular waist belt plates had been in use since 1827. The shoulder belt shown is for the bayonet which was worn on the left side. Since the original photograph was a mirror image, the corporal shifted the belt and cap box to their opposite sides in order for them to appear correct. Consequently, the shoulder belt seems to be for the cartridge box when it is not. Cap boxes were adopted when the Marine Corps converted to percussion rifles in around 1851 and its appearance here indicates the image was taken after that year. The significance of the brass slide below the oval plate is unknown and may have been a locally produced badge of merit. The two colour pompon is also unknown.

Below left: Enlisted men, regulation 1859 undress, USS *Kearsarge*, 1861. Though grainy, this detail from a larger image shows a portion of the Marine detachment on board the USS *Kearsarge*. The close fit of the coats, particularly the sleeves, indicates garments made before the Civil War as war-time images invariably show the wide sleeves and looser fit of Civil War period fashions. Also of interest is the lack of slings to the rifles, a pre-war practice.

Below: Orderly Sergeant James Buckner, c.1860. Changes in uniform were always a problem for ships' detachments that might be at sea when the change occurred and, consequently, might find themselves in an obsolete dress. The Quartermaster Department, therefore, attempted to provide the initial production of the 1859 uniform to detachments just then getting ready for sea. Delays in the manufacture of dress coats meant that these detachments only received a partial issue consisting of the single-breasted undress and fatigue uniforms. Orderly Sergeant Buckner commanded one of these detachments and, after receiving the undress coats, created an interim dress coat by attaching his epaulets from his old uniform coat. His cap was also unique to 1859. It has the oversized plate and brass pompon that were discontinued following the initial production contract. Caps made after 1859 had smaller front plates and carried red worsted pompons. (Photograph courtesy of John Buckner.)

Above: Second Lieutenant A. W. Ward, around 1863. The full sleeves and wide-legged trousers, fashionable during the 1860s, show up well in this image. Lieutenant Ward was in the undress uniform called for by the regulations. The similarity to the contemporary Army uniform was striking, but the uniform had several features unique to the Marine Corps. Its buttons carried the eagle-grasping-anchor device. The cap was the Chasseur-style kepi with a gold embroidered bugle horn on red cloth and bore an 'M' device within the loop, and black mohair braid to the sides and to the quatrefoil on top. All officer frock coats were double-breasted, a feature restricted to field grade officers

in the Army, and they carried Russian shoulder knots of gold cord on scarlet cloth as rank devices. Ward is without the gold sword-knot and this image was probably made while he was off-duty as the crimson sash is also missing.

Above: Second Lieutenant George Reid, c.1863. From the 1830s on, Marine officers were allowed a light jacket for fatigue. It was not, however, until the 1859 uniform changes that rank devices were added to this garment in the form of the undress gold cord shoulder knots. There is no known significance to the cuff design seen in the photograph and it was discontinued in 1875.

Right: Detail from a photograph of the Marine Corps Band and barrack guard, Marine Barracks Washington, D.C., spring 1864. This close-up shows the guard detachment commander, Captain Lucien Dawson, and Sergeant Major Frederick Cook. Captain Dawson was in undress but has on the white dress belt instead of the black leather belt. The sergeant major's uniform was as prescribed in regulations for staff non-commissioned officers but with the addition of gold Prussian lace to the collar, cuffs, and chevrons. His epaulets were also gold and clearly show in the photograph. As a staff noncommissioned officer, Sergeant Major Cook did not carry a musket.

Left: Director of the Marine Band, Francis Scala, around 1865. The British Army prescribed specially designed uniform coats laced in gold for regimental staff non-commissioned officers and the practice was subsequently adopted by the Army and Marine Corps. Consequently, the sergeant major, the quartermaster sergeant and the band director of the Marine Corps, wore a combination of officer and enlisted uniform items. Francis Scala's scarlet coat followed the design prescribed for enlisted dress coats but it was trimmed with gold Prussian lace instead of yellow worsted. The coat's collar and cuffs were edged in white. His epaulets were almost identical to the pattern stipulated for second lieutenants but with a very narrow fringe. The dress cap has the officers' drooping feather plume. Scala's sash was crimson silk net as prescribed for staff non-commissioned officers.

Above: Private Allen Bronson, 1870. Private Bronson has on what may well be the third pattern coat. It resembled the second pattern but had a shortened collar with only one loop bearing a button at each end. The 1859 epaulets worn by Marines consisted of a brass shoulder scale with detachable yellow worsted fringe.

Above right: Unidentified Marine private, dress uniform with undress cap, 1875–92. The enlisted dress coat, introduced in May 1875, had a better fit than its predecessor. It was identical to the musicians' coat but of dark blue cloth trimmed with yellow lace on a scarlet ground. Brass scales with yellow fringe completed the coat. This is one of the earliest photographs of an enlisted man wearing the eagle-globe-and-anchor device adopted in 1868 to replace the bugle horn. The new insignia incorporated the pre-1859 eagle-and-anchor cap plate with the English Royal Marine globe to create an entirely new symbol; an elegant design and one that came to embody the Marine Corps itself.

Right: Second Lieutenant William Zeilin, fatigue dress, around 1876. Lieutenant Zeilin was the son of Brigadier General Jacob Zeilin, seventh Commandant of the Marine Corps. Lieutenant Zeilin is wearing a non-standard fatigue dress. Second lieutenants had the same uniform as first lieutenants but without specific rank insignia. The officer quatrefoil can be seen on top of the kepi. This device continues in use to the present on the officers' service and dress caps. According to legend, the quatrefoil originated from Marines attaching a twisted rope to the top of their caps so that snipers stationed in the tops could tell friend from foe in a melee. In reality, the quatrefoil had been a feature of French officer caps since the 1830s, and became a part of Marine officer dress when the kepi was adopted in 1859.

Above: Marine Guard, dress uniform, USS *Lancaster*, 1883. The smartness of the Marine uniform was in marked contrast with the loose fit of the Navy enlisted uniform. The Marine officer's gold laced, French-style uniform cap, with its drooping scarlet feather plume, is in contrast to the plainness of the enlisted cap. Note that the officer, and many of the enlisted, is wearing the cap slightly tipped to the right. In 1875, the Mameluke sword was re-established for officers.

Below: Enlisted men, undress, with overcoats, around 1888. The sky blue overcoat was being worn without the detachable cape. Note the chevrons on the non-commissioned officers' lower sleeves.

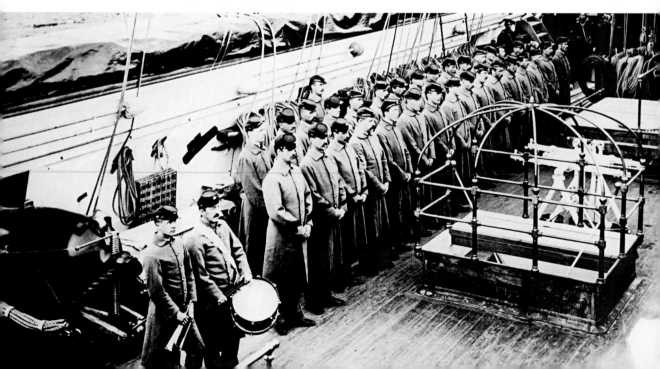

Above: Marine detachment, undress, Naval Academy, Annapolis, 1889. This image is one of the earliest photographs to show Marines wearing knapsacks. The occasion depicted is unknown, but the knapsack with rolled overcoat was, since 1798, the basic sea-going kit carried by guard detachments going aboard ship. Other field equipment such as haversacks and canteens were not issued to these detachments as they seldom served far from their ships. Marine and Army fatigue dress were similar at this time; however, the Marine coat had a small standing collar, shoulder straps and red piping to collar, cuffs and shoulder stripes. Marine chevrons and service stripes continued to be yellow worsted lace on a scarlet ground.

Right: Colonel Commandant Charles Heywood (front row, centre), undress, 1894. In the uniform regulations of 1892, the fatigue coat was redesignated as undress and reduced-size eagle-globe-and-anchor devices were added to the collar next to the officer's rank insignia. In addition, the commandant's cap device was distinguished by a wreath of gold acorn leaves as seen here. The sleeves of the commandant's coat have the points-up chevron with tracing braid denoting field grade rank while the two company grade officers have the Austrian knot. The second lieutenant (rear right) is distinguished by the lack of a rank device on the collar as compared to the first lieutenant on the left.

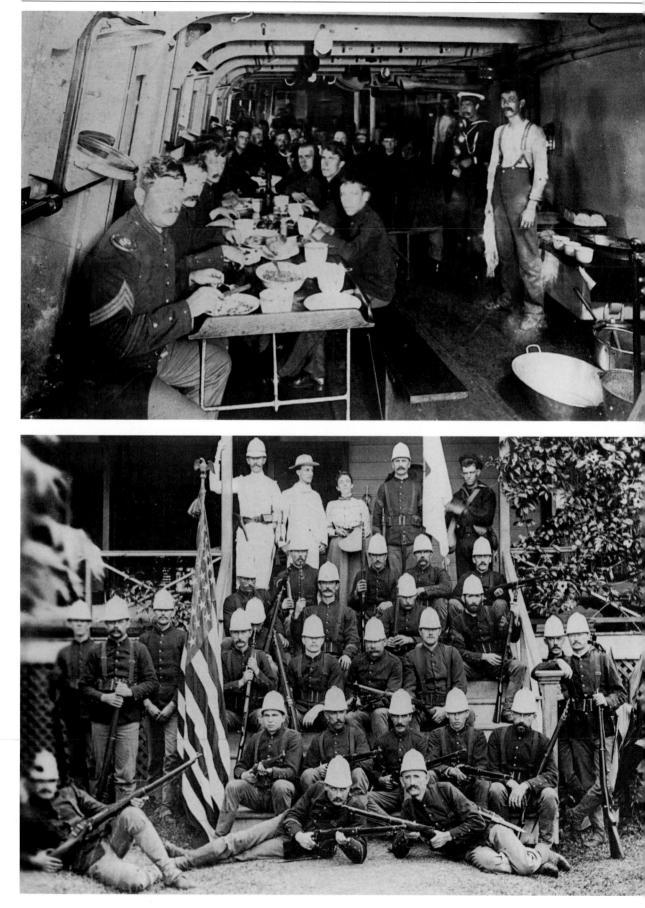

Opposite page, top: Marine ship's detachment, dress and undress, USS *Galena*, around 1900. The sergeant on the left is wearing dress uniform with its distinctive red cord shoulder knots whilst the boy musician has on the undress coat.

Opposite page, bottom: Marine detachment, undress, at the home of the United States Consul, Matautu Point, Samoa, April 1899. Improvements in weaponry occurred rapidly during the 1890s and into the next century. These Marines carry the bolt-action M1895 Lee straight-pull rifles and wear dark blue web cartridge belts with shoulder straps issued in

1895. Top left, the officer commanding the detachment wears the hot weather and summer undress uniform with black leather pistol and sword belt. White summer helmets were adopted in 1891.

Above: Marines and sailors, Camp McCulla, Guantanamo, Cuba, 15 June 1898. After much of the fighting had ended, sailors from the fleet, such as the two on the right, volunteered for land duty in order to relieve the Marines after they seized Guantanamo. Khaki field service dress was not available to the Marines so white linen summer undress was used instead.

Lieutenant Colonel Richard Collum, dress, around 1904. From 1904 to 1922, officers on the staff were to wear a single-breasted coat with shoulder knots and staff aiguillette. Line officers had double-breasted coats and epaulets. Major Collum's grade insignia consisted of a silver embroidered oak leaf on a scarlet ground.

Colonel Harry White, special full dress, around 1910. The field grade officers' dress coat differed from company grade officers' by the use of British-style gold lace chevron with tracing braided cuff, the heavy bullion fringe to the epaulet and the embroidered visor. Colonel White's cap has a rare early version of visor embroidery. The use of epaulets was specified for 'special full dress'.

Left: Enlisted service dress, around 1914. The enlisted summer field service uniform differed from the winter service uniform in colour and pattern. Made of khaki cotton for summer, the coat was single-breasted with pointed cuffs, had five bronze buttons, a standing collar without collar devices and two pleated patch pockets on the breast. There were no pockets on the skirts. Matching cotton trousers were worn along with canvas leggings for certain duties. When worn with leggings, the trouser legs were carefully folded below the knee and presented an almost smooth and fitted look. Initially full-size off-white coloured chevrons were used but were replaced by small-size chevrons of forest green on khaki twill. This figure has the M1903 Springfield rifle with bayonet and 1907 cartridge belt. The 1912 uniform was worn with minor modifications until replaced by the rolled collar version in 1927.

Opposite page, top: Marine guard, ship's detachment, dress, c.1910. The gold laced and double-breasted officers' dress uniform was in marked contrast to the comparatively less ornate scarlet trimmed single-breasted uniform worn by enlisted men. The use of knots on the officers' coats signifies full dress.

Opposite page, bottom: Marine gun crew, summer undress, USS *Pennsylvania*, around 1914. The improved lines of the dress and undress coat can be seen in the figures here. On the extreme right, the coat's tailoring shows a slight outward push to the skirts at the junction of the waist and back panel seams. The use of inch wide trouser stripes was extended to corporals in 1912.

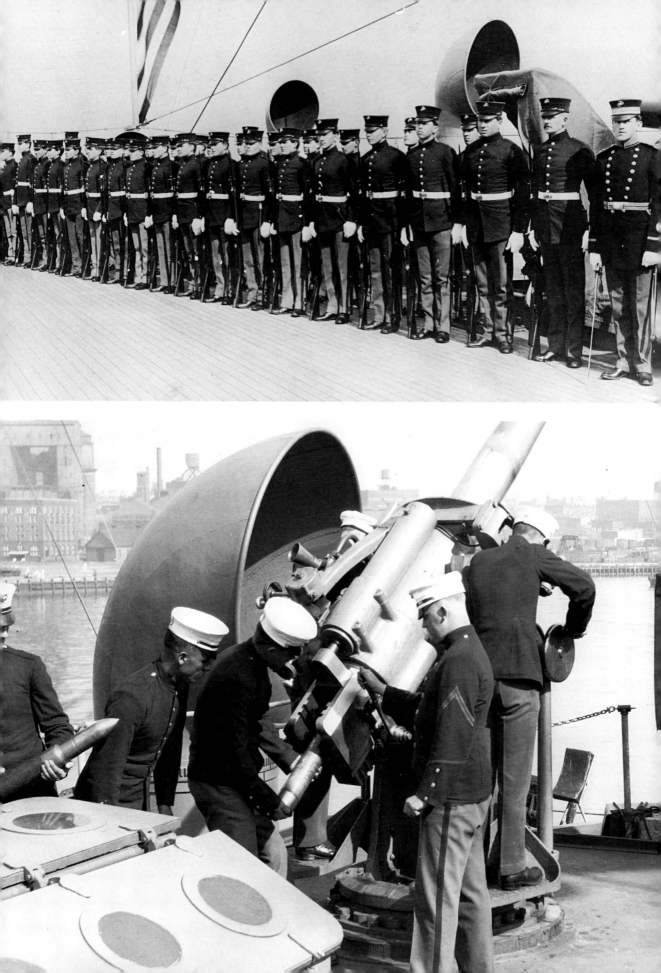

Opposite page, top: Officers and staff non-commissioned officer, field service dress, Vera Cruz, Mexico, during the occupation of that city by United States forces in 1914. This group included some of the more prominent Marines of the early twentieth century: (from left to right) Captain F. DeLano, Sergeant Major John Quick (Medal of Honor recipient), Lieutenant Colonel William Neville (future commandant), Colonel John Lejeune (future commandant) and Major Smedley Butler (twice recipient of the Medal of Honor). The officers are wearing tan cotton breeches with russet leather shoes, leggings and pistol belts; Sergeant Major Quick has straight-legged khaki cotton trousers bloused into canvas leggings. Though the Army adopted the Montana peaked campaign hat some years before, the Marine Corps did not move to the new hat until the 1912 uniform changes. Even so, the old style continued in use until 1914 and Marines at Vera Cruz wore both types, as shown in this group. A bronze eagle-globe-and-anchor device was positioned on the front of both campaign hats and officers had cords to their hats as well.

Opposite page, bottom: Enlisted men, field service dress, Quantico, Virginia, June 1916. In marked contrast to the USS Pennsylvania's gun crew, these field artillerymen have on drab summer field service dress. The khaki flannel shirt was introduced in 1904 and worn throughout the First World War. Small-size forest-green chevrons on khaki were worn on the sleeves. The private first class in the foreground has moved his left arm clear of the gun's recoil and is about to use the right hand, behind his back, to pull the firing lanyard.

Top left: Lieutenant, summer service uniform, c.1914. The characteristic short skirts of the regulation 1912 summer service coat is apparent. This officer has on boots instead of shoes and leggings.

Above: Brigadier General Littleton Waller, about 1917, wearing the dress uniform prescribed for his rank. The most notable rank features are the grouping of buttons by two, the absence of the cuff flap and the single star on the epaulet. By 1917, personal decorations and medals were to be mounted in groups of three on medal bars that passed between the front and back ribbons. His medals included, on the top row right, the rare Specially Meritorious Medal conferred upon officers and men of the Navy and Marine Corps for meritorious service other than in battle during the Spanish–American War. Only 93 known awards were given making it one of the rarest American decorations.

Above: Marine Gunner Henry Hulbert, winter service dress, December 1917. The National Defense Act of August 1916 authorized the warrant officer grades of marine gunner and quartermaster clerk. Again following British practice, warrant officers in the Marine Corps wore a variation of officer dress. Marine Gunner Hulbert has the regulation 1912 winter field service uniform with English-pattern Sam Browne belt, typical of officer dress in the European theatre of operations, but his collar lacks the eagle-globe-and-anchor device. In its place, he has the 'bursting bomb' insignia of his specialty and grade.

Above: Officer, winter field service dress with cloak, 1918. The cloak worn by this unidentified officer resembles the regulation boat cloak of dark blue broadcloth lined in scarlet used with the dress and undress uniforms. A field service cloak was not prescribed and this is the only known photograph of one being worn. It had a large stand-and-fall collar and closed with four bronze coat buttons. Judging from the frayed button-holes, this cloak had been worn quite often. The officer's Army-style overseas cap appears to be devoid of insignia.

Left: Privates First Class Mary Kelly, May O'Keefe and Ruth Spike, winter field service dress, Headquarters Marine Corps, Washington, D.C., 1918. Women were enlisted in the Marine Corps Reserve to free male Marines for overseas duty. The winter field service dress provided for them should have used the same forest green wool as the male version, but it was actually made of olive drab wool. Women's coats had a roll-collar and buttoned on the left. The front was closed by four large-size bronze Marine buttons and the pockets were the same as on the male winter field service garment. Again, as with the male enlisted version, no collar device was prescribed. The cap specified for women was the 'glengarry' style used by the British Army. This cap carried the enlisted bronze hat and cap device on the left side.

Right: Major General John Lejeune, winter service dress, winter 1918-19. General Lejeune's silver stars were embroidered directly to the straps of the forest green winter service coat; on his left sleeve is the 'Indianhead' patch of the 2nd Infantry Division. The box-pleat, characteristic of Marine uniform coats after 1912, is clearly shown as is the pocket flap's single button. Army officer coats had the three-pointed scalloped flap. Though the visors of field grade and general officer frame caps were embroidered, the visors of field service caps were plain for all officers.

Above: Officers, field service dress, France, 18 June 1918. Surviving officers of the 2nd Battalion, 6th Marine Regiment, posed for this photograph after the Belleau Wood campaign. They are wearing a variety of uniform items ranging from the regulation forest green wool service dress and privately purchased trench coats to Army puttees, leggings and lace-up boots. Several have their shirt collars pulled over the coat's high standing collar to reduce it rubbing the neck, a common practice with Army and Marine officers.

Left: Enlisted man, Army field service dress, 1918. On 10 January 1918, General John Pershing, the AEF (Army Expeditionary Force) commander, decided to simplify American logistical requirements by putting Marines in the Army M1912 service dress. This uniform lacked Marine insignia until an Army-style circular collar disk bearing the eagle-globe-and-anchor emblem was introduced in August 1918, at the urging of the then Assistant Secretary of the Navy, Franklin Delano Roosevelt. The collar disk marked the first use of the Marine emblem on the enlisted uniform. Canvas leggings also ceased to be worn by Marines in the AEF and were replaced by Army olive drab puttees.

Above: Machine-gun crew, winter 1918–19. Photographed during the march to the Rhine, these two Marines show some of the modifications that occurred to their dress after landing in France and assignment to the Army Expeditionary Force. They have puttees instead of canvas leggings and the Army-issue overcoat lacks the pointed cuff. Both Marines appear to have shortened the skirts of their coats leaving a rough and uneven edge. They have on the 1910 field pack with web belt, 1910 first aid pouch, and both the M1912 dismounted holster and the M1916 holster for the M1911 .45 calibre automatic pistol. The machine gun being carried was the M1917 Browning watercooled with tripod base, issued to Marine units in November 1918.

Right: Captain Robert Lytle, non-regulation aviation overcoat, late 1918. Captain Lytle served in the First Marine Aviation Force and led the first all-Marine Corps bombing raid in the war. He has on a brown leather, knee-length aviators' overcoat with belt and three large pockets (two patch pockets on the skirts and one internal pocket on the upper left breast) made by Spalding Aviation Equipment. Captain Lytle has no rank insignia on the overcoat's shoulder straps and the overseas cap lacks the Marine Corps emblem but has the officers' collar-size rank device.

Above: Officers, field dress, winter 1918–19. The conditions of the Western Front took their toll on uniformity. The right-hand figure, in a non-regulation trench coat, has the 2nd Division patch and Army-issue puttees instead of the prescribed leather leggings seen on the centre figure. The officer on the left has high-topped lace-up boots closed by three straps and buckles. Both he and the officer in the centre are wearing the officers' version of the Marine regulation 1912 forest green overcoat. The overcoat was short-waisted and double-breasted with five bronze Marine buttons in each row. Note that the centre figure is missing a button on the left row and that he has the Army-style wool overseas cap with the eagle-globe-and-anchor emblem on the right side. The right-hand figure does not appear to be wearing any rank insignia and may be an enlisted man.

Left: Marine lieutenant, winter field service dress, France, autumn 1917. The regulation 1912 winter field uniform for officers followed the style of the blue undress coat but was forest green with bronze buttons and collar insignia. This image depicts the appearance of Marine officers soon after landing in France and before the Sam Browne belt was adopted there. The Sam Browne belt was not formally prescribed for all officers until 1921. The ribbed band on the officers' winter field cap had a lighter appearance than the forest green crown but was in fact the same colour. Enlisted caps did not have ribbed bands. The lieutenant has the Expert Marksman badge over his left breast pocket as per regulations. Officers wore matching forest green breeches and russet leather leggings with this coat.

Right: Ambulance driver, field service dress, summer 1917, Quantico, Virginia. In 1917, Elizabeth Pearce presented the regiments going to France with several Ford-built ambulances, known subsequently as 'Elizabeth Fords', a term that later evolved into 'Tin Lizzie' in reference to mass produced Ford automobiles. The private in summer field service dress shows the distinctive cut of the Marine flannel shirt. Army-issue shirts were pull-over and only buttoned part of the way down the front. This photograph shows the web belt adopted in 1904. The belt and brass buckle have remained in use to the present.

Below: Enlisted men, 3-inch anti-aircraft gun training, summer 1917. The corporal and the left hand figure are wearing flannel shirts of a lighter shade than the khaki worn by the other Marines. Each member of the gun crew has the improved M1910 cartridge belt with the c.1915 snap closures. Note the fold behind the left figure's knee produced when blousing trousers or leggings. Two Marines are equipped with the standard Army canteen, however, the enlisted man in the centre has the unique Marine Corps-issued canteen cover.

Left: Gunnery Sergeant Daniel Daly, winter dress uniform, around 1919. Gunnery Sergeant Daly received a second Medal of Honor and an Army Distinguished Service Cross for actions in France. The chevron designating a gunnery sergeant consisted of three yellow stripes with crossed rifles behind a bursting bomb.

Below: Inspection of the Marine ship's detachment, summer service dress, around 1922. Service caps with the wide flared crown began to replace the old-style cap after the First World War. Some Marines in the formation have on the new cap. Compare the appearance of this formation with the USS *Missouri*'s honour guard in September 1945.

Opposite page: Lieutenant, intermediate weather winter field service dress, 1930s, watercolour by Colonel Magruder USMC. The lieutenant is depicted in the typical field uniform for officers worn during the inter-war period. He has the Marine Corps version of the Army's M1912 dismounted holster. The khaki, square-cut field scarf or tie was similar to the Army version, although Marines wore it with the ends outside the shirt, as shown, while the Army required it to be tucked between the first and second buttons. Swagger sticks were favoured by Marine officers from the First World War to the 1960s when they gradually went out of use.

Above: Captain James Davis and Lieutenant Christian Schilt, flight dress, Nicaragua, 1920. In the early years of marine aviation, flight clothing was not standardized.

Left: Commandant John A. Lejeune, winter undress, 1927. Major General Lejeune's coat has the longer skirts and larger pockets introduced after 1917. The shift of his Sam Browne belt reveals the bottom button, later replaced by a flat plastic button when the cloth belt came into use following the Second World War. The wreath, surrounding the cap emblem, was only authorized for the commandant.

Right: Commandant of the Marine Corps John A. Lejeune in winter field service dress with unidentified general officers in undress with boatcloaks, around 1927. The Sam Browne belt was prescribed for all officers in 1921 and it continued in use until 1942. It was revived in the 1960s for certain posts and stations. General Lejeune's belt was the English-made one he acquired in 1918. The belt worn by the officer on the right has the wide frame buckle characteristic of the current style. The boatcloak shown was the 1900 pattern which is still authorized. It was made of navy-blue broadcloth edged with black mohair braid. The collar was black velvet and a black silk loop *à echelle* went from the left shoulder to a black silk frog button on the right shoulder. Four black buttons closed the cloak through a concealed flap on the left side. The lining was scarlet.

Below: Enlisted men, Peking Legation Mounted Detachment, winter field service dress, Peking, China, 1936. The mounted detachment was formed to increase the legation guard's mobility. Although riding diminutive Asian horses, the detachment was fully equipped as cavalry to include the Army M1913 Cavalry sabre. The Marines of this squad were wearing the enlisted coat introduced about 1926–28 and have a secondary chin strap to their service caps. They display two styles of marksmanship badges. The Army-style on the left hand figure was introduced in 1922 but never supplanted the earlier badge (right and second from right figures) and was phased out by 1941.

Above: Captain Ford Rogers, Lieutenant Colonel Ross Rowell and First Lieutenant William McKittrick, summer field dress, Quantico, Virginia, around 1933. Lieutenant Colonel Rowell was notable for having led the first organized dive bombing attack against insurgents in Santo Domingo in 1928. By the 1930s, breeches had acquired a pronounced flair. Officer ties were either square cut or pointed and their footwear included boots as well as the earlier shoes and leggings, as seen being worn by Captain Rogers on the left.

Left: Captain Louis Cukela, blue evening dress, around 1932. In October 1921, the mess jacket was redesigned and shoulder knots with rank insignia and dress collar-size eagle-globe-and-anchor devices were prescribed for wear with this garment. Captain Cukela's rank was further indicated by tracing braid around the Austrian sleeve knot. Captain Cukela has the Navy 'Tiffany' version, designed by the Tiffany Company, of the Medal of Honor suspended from the neck and the Army Medal of Honor in miniature with his other decorations. The fourragère is being worn incorrectly, with the braided cord over rather than under the arm.

Above: Major General Smedly Butler and Commandant of the Marine Corps, Major General Neville, winter service dress, Quantico, Virginia, around 1930. General Neville, on the right, died a short time after this visit to Quantico. The officers' version of the roll-collar winter service dress had longer skirts than the enlisted garment. Both have early pattern Sam Browne belts of English pattern. General Butler's shirt was khaki with a khaki necktie and has the collar closed by a collar pin while General Neville has on a white shirt and a black necktie.

Right: Captain Merritt Edson, winter field service dress, about 1931. Future recipient of the Medal of Honor, Merritt Edson was one of several aviators who would earn notoriety as ground commanders in the Second World War. His uniform has the 1924 pattern eagle-globe-and-anchor characterized by the drooping rather than upswept wings of the collar insignia. Edson's decorations include the Navy Cross, the Navy Distinguished Service Medal and the Distinguished Marksman badge. The squared buckle on the Sam Browne's shoulder strap was favoured by Marine officers during the late 1920s and the 1930s.

Above: Enlisted men, 6th Marine Regiment, winter service dress, Iceland, 1941. Service dress was still considered a field uniform in 1941. As part of American pre-war assistance to Britain, the 1st Marine Brigade (Provisional) took over the garrisoning of Iceland from the British 49th Division. On the suggestion of the division commander, the brigade adopted the division's Polar Bear shoulder patch and wore it until the brigade's return to California in 1942. Photographed while shopping in Reykjavik, the Marine on the left has the fourragère indicative of the 6th Marine Regiment. The coat was the pattern adopted 1926–28 and worn with the enlisted garrison belt. Both the winter forest green service cap and garrison cap could be worn with this uniform. The small-size bronze collar emblem was used with the garrison cap.

Left: Captain Robert Blake and Private First Class Ralph Zanga, utility uniform, New Georgia Island, Central Solomons, summer 1943. The two-piece, sage green, utility uniform appeared in late 1941 as a replacement for the blue denim work uniform. It was not intended for field service but by 1942 it was coming under increasing use as the standard combat dress. Made of herring-bone-twill, the upper left breast pocket featured a black stencilled Marine Corps 1936-style eagle-globe-and-anchor with the 'USMC' legend. It was worn both inside and outside the trousers as shown here. Collar emblems were not authorized with this uniform but were sometimes worn nevertheless. The right hand figure has the fair-leather waist belt developed for Defense Battalions used as a pistol belt. The M1 helmets lack the reversible camouflage covers that appeared in autumn 1943.

Above: Enlisted men, summer field service dress, Montford Point, North Carolina, 1943. The Marine Corps began to enlist African-Americans in June 1942 but followed the contemporary practice of organizing them into racially segregated units under white officers. Since there was no history of African-Americans in the Marine Corps, there was no pool of experienced enlisted men with which to create a cadre of black sergeants and corporals. Promising enlistees were given special training, promoted, and made drill instructors. As a drill instructor, Corporal Edgar Huff, future sergeant major, wore winter service dress and is seen training a recruit platoon in intermediate weather summer service dress.

Right: Private First Class Peter Nahaidinae, Private First Class Joseph Gatewood, and Corporal Lloyd Oliver, 1st Marine Division, Southwest Pacific, 1944. The Marine Corps enlisted Navajo Indians as radiomen. Speaking in their native language, radio communications proved impossible for the Japanese to decipher. Nahaidinae and Gatewood wore the pattern 1944 camouflaged herring-bone-twill utility uniform closed by oxidized bronze or blackened steel dome snaps. This posed photograph, taken during a training exercise, shows two men with hand painted helmet liners without the steel outer shell M1 helmet. Corporal Oliver, on the right, is dressed in the sage green pattern 1941 herring-bone-twill utility uniform displaying the three-pocket arrangement and 1936-style emblem on the upper left pocket. The forest green garrison cap with bronze Marine collar emblem could be worn with the utility uniform.

Left: Enlisted man, utility uniform, 1945, after twelve days of fighting. Typical late war dress consisting of very worn pattern 1941 utility uniform with the 1943 reversible camouflage helmet cover and the rough-out field shoes or 'Boondockers'.

Right: Captain Helen O'Neill, winter service uniform, about 1945. The winter service uniform for women Marines, designed by Mainbocher, was made of forest green material and used the same buttons and emblems as the male service uniform. Her service cap has scarlet cords.

Lower right: Colonel Herman Hannekan, field service dress, 1st Marine Division, Australia, November 1943. Shortages of Marine Corps service dress clothing led to issue of Australian 'battle jackets' to the 1st and 2nd Marine Divisions while training in Australia. Made of brownish olive drab colour, with a stronger red cast than Marine forest green, the coat resembled the British battledress but with buttoned cuff tabs. The collar was pressed open for wear with the khaki shirt and tie. This style garment proved popular with Allied forces and was adopted by the American Army and referred to as the 'Ike' jacket in honour of General of the Army Dwight Eisenhower. The Marine version was in forest green with Marine buttons on the cuff and was known as the 'Vandegrift' jacket after General Alexander Vandegrift, commanding general of the 1st Marine Division at the time the jackets were first issued. Khaki summer service trousers and garrison cap were worn with this garment. Colonel Hannekan's jacket lacks the bronze collar emblems that could have been worn but he has the formation patch of the 1st Marine Division on his upper left sleeve and the silver eagles on the shoulder straps. His ribbons include the Medal of Honor, two Navy Crosses, a Silver Star and a Presidential Unit Citation. Each row of ribbons was seperately attached on its own bar.

Above: Flight personnel, summer service, Pacific theatre, around 1943. The enlisted man on the right has on the khaki garrison cap and a shortened utility shirt. On the left, the officer has on the khaki summer service uniform typical of flight personnel. His cap is from a civilian baseball club.

Left: Enlisted men, Cape Gloucester, early 1944. The M1942 Army-made camouflage one piece jungle suit worn by these two Marines proved unsuitable for jungle fighting. The top could not be removed but had to be rolled down as done here.

Left: Sergeant Robert Martin, utility dress, Peleliu, Caroline archipelago, autumn 1944. Sergeant Martin sounded 'To the Colors', as the United States flag was raised on Peleliu. By 1944, the second pattern camouflage cover had reached Marines in the Pacific. Sergeant Martin has one of the new patterns which was characterized by slits cut into the fabric for attaching foliage. He has the skirts of his sage green utility coat tucked into his pattern 1941 utility trousers, a practice which became standardized in the post-war years and led to the design of the M1952 utility coat. Note that Sergeant Martin is wearing his issue field service shoes, 'boondockers', in the regulation manner with the 1936 pattern khaki canvas field leggings issued to all Marines. The single-piston bugle was a type usually reserved for drum and bugle corps.

Right: Second Lieutenant Elizabeth McKinnon, summer service undress, Camp Lejeune, North Carolina, June 1944. Photographed soon after graduation from officer candidate school, Lieutenant McKinnon has on the long-sleeved undress uniform jacket with matching skirt of green and white striped seersucker material prescribed for wear off-duty. This uniform could be worn in place of the white summer dress uniform which was an optional purchase. Both the gilt dress and bronze service Marine Corps emblems were authorized with this uniform. Lieutenant McKinnon's cap was the prescribed summer dress cap of pale green material with white cord and silver-gilt Marine cap emblem. The officer cap emblem was of two-piece construction having a separately applied 'fouling' rope distinct from the less pronounced rope on the enlisted one-piece version. The 'fouling' rope was omitted from both enlisted and officer collar emblems.

Above: Honour guard of the USS *Missouri*, summer service dress, Tokyo Bay, 2 September 1945. The guard awaits the arrival of the Japanese representatives. Dressed in khaki summer service, this unit displays the scarlet shoulder patch with a yellow sea horse over a blue anchor used to designate ships' detachments. Note the distinctive saddle to the crown of the enlisted service cap.

Left: Major General Pedro Del Valle, winter service dress, 1945. Major General Del Valle has the formation patch of the 1st Marine Division on his left sleeve. The patch consisted of a blue diamond with white stars and a red '1'. His ribbons, which included the Navy Cross, Legion of Merit with star, Navy Marine Corps Medal and Presidential Unit Citation, were the large-size (½ inch wide) style prescribed for Navy and Marine personnel. The Army and Army Air Force used a narrower bar. Each bar on the General's coat was separately attached and the number of ribbons on some bars were reduced from four to three to one in order to avoid being covered by the lapel.

Right: Enlisted men, summer service and overalls, Iwo Jima, 1945. Posed in front of their Army developed DUKW amphibious truck, used for hauling cargo ashore and carrying out wounded, these African-American Marines have on a mix of utility clothing, sage green overalls and summer service dress.

Below: Private First Class Alfred Roy, winter service dress with field jacket, Peking, China, late 1945. Alfred Roy has a newly issued Army M1943 field jacket over his forest green winter service dress with overseas cap.

Below right: Private First Class Clyde Pelletier, utility uniform, Sasebo, Japan, 28 September 1945. Pelletier has on a pattern 1941 utility coat tucked into his trousers, scarlet and yellow 'MP' brassard, an M1 helmet liner and light brown field service shoes without leggings.

Above: Colonel Katherine Towle, evening dress, Washington, D.C., 17 November 1950. Colonel Towle was the first post-war Director of Women Marines. She has on the new evening dress uniform designed by Mainbocher and adopted on 9 November, in time for her to wear it to the 175th birthday of the Marine Corps the next day.

Top left: Lieutenant Robert Lucy, utility uniform, Korea, 30 August 1950. The distinctive 1936 emblem continued in use into the 1950s. Lieutenant Lucy has chosen to wear the utility coat with the skirts tucked in the waist band.

Lower left: Enlisted men, cold weather utility uniform, Korea, 1951. The herring-bone-twill sage green utility cap, introduced in 1941, featured a short visor while the 1944 version, which remains in use, had a longer visor and stiffeners in the front of the crown, as seen on the left.

Right: Enlisted man, cold weather combat dress, Washington, D.C., 14 November 1950. Dressed for field service in cold weather, this Marine illustrates the layering concept: no single garment can keep the individual warm, but in the right combination could be very effective. In this case, the Marine has on a triple-ply M1943 cotton field jacket and trousers over a woollen high-neck sweater, flannel shirt, woollen service trousers and woollen long underwear.

Left: Sergeant Margaret Dill, summer uniform, Quantico Boat Club, Quantico, Virginia, around 1958. The matching cap, jacket and skirt were made of a light green (green and white stripes) nylon-Dacron cord fabric. It had shoulder straps and cuffs edged in dark green cord. All buttons and emblem devices were black.

Below: Lieutenant Colonel Albert Schoepper, Director of the United States Marine Band, full dress, Marine Barracks, Washington, D.C., 7 July 1958. The band uniform has been described separately since 1797. The position of Band Leader was unique in its evolution from staff non-comissioned officer to staff full officer status. The pattern of chest braiding dated to the 1870s and, aside from cuff ornamentation, remained virtually unchanged from the design adopted in 1892.

Opposite page, top: Officers, 5th Marines, utility uniform, Korea, about 1951. The officer second from right has on 1944 pattern utilities which were produced too late for general use during the Second World War. The large breast pocket was for maps or grenades. Leggings were worn by Marines into the 1950s. The M1943 field jackets were the same as worn by the Army, but with the Marine emblem and 'USMC' stencilled on the left pocket. The officer second from right has on Army field boots, and three of the four have the utility cap on underneath their helmets.

Opposite page bottom: Major John Glenn, Jr., flight dress, Korea, 25 March 1953. Wearing a leather G.I. jacket over his flight suit, the future astronaut examines damage to the tail of his F9F Panther jet.

Above: Corporal Richard Milton, 'I' Company, 3rd Battalion, 3rd Marines, Tri Binh Province, Vietnam, 19 September 1965. In this first year of Marine Corps involvement in Vietnam, the M14 was the standard weapon in use. Dressed for patrol, Corporal Milton wears the helmet liner in lieu of the steel outer shell and has on the dark green rain coat over his utilities. He is not wearing a flak jacket.

Below: Enlisted men, 3rd Reconnaissance Battalion, 29 July 1965. First pattern tropical utility uniform is seen on the corporal, second left, and the extreme right hand figures. The corporal has subdued rank insignia on the collar. Some also have subdued insignia on the front of their caps.

Above: Enlisted men, 3rd Marine Division, Vietnam, 1966. The two Marines stand perimeter guard with an M-60 machine-gun. The gunner has cut off most of the sleeves of his coat.

Right: Marine officer, Vietnam, 8 November 1966. The second pattern tropical combat uniform had the buttons concealed beneath the pocket flaps to prevent snagging. Officers dispensed with rank insignia completely, or wore it in some inconspicuous place, such as under the pocket flap.

Above: Drill instructor and recruit, Parris Island, South Carolina, 1967. The drill instructor is dressed in summer service uniform with distinctive waistbelt, brass eagle-globe-and-anchor belt plate, and 'DI' hat. Running with poncho and full duffle bag, the private, or 'boot', has on the ubiquitous silver-painted helmet liner worn by all recruits.

Opposite page, top: Private First Class Howard Oakley, 3rd Battalion, 5th Marines, combat uniform, 30 November 1968. The cloth helmet cover was printed with a camouflage

pattern that was reversible, with green for spring and summer and brown for autumn and winter.

Opposite page, bottom: Lieutenant Miles Davis (centre) being promoted to first lieutenant by his father, Major General Raymond Davis (right), commanding general, 3rd Marine Division, and Colonel Robert Barrow, Vietnam, 1969. All three officers wear the third pattern all-cotton ERDL camouflage tropical combat uniform.

Below: Enlisted men, jungle utility uniform, 3rd Reconnaissance Battalion, Con Thien, Vietnam, 2 February 1969. Based on the design of the Second World War Army parachutist uniform, the camouflage jungle version had four bellows pockets.

Opposite page, top: Enlisted men, 3rd Battalion, 26th Marines, tropical combat uniform, 14 January 1970. Equipped for a lengthy patrol, these Marines are wearing the ERDL camouflage combat uniform, fragmentation protective vests, or flak jackets, and M1 steel helmets.

Opposite page, bottom: Captain Dolores Noguara, summer service, Marine Corps Air Station Quantico, Virginia, August 1968. Throughout the 1960s, and into the 1970s, the Women Marines' summer service uniform continued to be light green with dark green edging to cuffs, shoulder straps and collar. The black buttons and collar emblems used with this uniform were identical for male and female dress. Women marines could wear their hair according to fashion, except when in uniform, when their hair had to be above the collar.

Enlisted men, jungle utilities, 3rd Marine Division, Vietnam, around 1969. In order to enhance mobility, reconnaissance
Marines going on patrol did not wear the helmet and flak jacket.

Enlisted man, utility uniform with flak jacket, Vietnam, 14 January 1970. Radiomen were a favourite target for snipers and many took care to conceal the radio set inside the backpack and to leave only the hand set exposed. This Marine has on the M55 armoured vest. The rope cording on the right shoulder prevented the M16A1 rifle from slipping to one side when being fired. Extra ammunition was carried in the cotton cloth bandoleer.

Above: Commandant of the Marine Corps, General Louis Wilson, summer service 'C' (Charlie) uniform, Camp Lejeune, North Carolina, 8 August 1975. The short sleeved khaki shirt was introduced after the Korean War. Marine dress regulations prescribed the wearing of ribbons on the shirt whenever the service coat was not being worn. Ribbons could either reflect all personal, campaign, and service medals rated by the Marine, or just personal decorations alone. General Wilson, a Medal of Honor recipient, chose in this instance to wear only the ribbons representing personal decorations. The practice of pressing vertical creases on the shirt began in the 1950s.

Left: Enlisted men, utility uniform, 155mm Howitzer, 'L' Battery, 3rd Battalion, 10th Marine Regiment, 2nd Marine Division, Camp Lejeune, North Carolina, 14 May 1975. Post-Korean War clothing developments by the Army produced the cotton olive green utility uniform that would remain in use for over two decades. The Marine utility top was identical to those provided for Army soldiers but it lacked sew-on name tags. Instead, the Marine emblem and 'USMC' was worn on the left pocket as before.

Right: Enlisted men, utility uniform, weapons platoon, 1st Battalion, 3rd Marines, Pakalula training area, Hawaii. Demonstrating the M47 Dragon Medium Anti-Tank/Assault Weapon, these Marines wear the camouflage utility uniform, commonly referred to as the 'woodland pattern', that replaced the olive green uniform in 1978. The new utility jacket had four pockets and was worn with the skirts outside the trousers.

Below: Marine fire fighting detail, utility uniform, California, 1970s. Other than the yellow jackets and helmets, the olive green utility uniform and standard equipment were used for all field activities.

Top right: Enlisted men, utility uniform with field protective masks, Recruit Depot, Parris Island, South Carolina, 26 October 1981. The underside of the camouflage material did not show the camouflage pattern. The Marine practice was to roll up the sleeves with the 'white' side out, while the Army practice was to roll the sleeves in such a way that the cuff covered the roll for a 'green' side out appearance. In extremely hot weather, the trousers were not bloused.

Bottom right: Enlisted man, green camouflage utility dress, 1982. By the late 1970s the green camouflage utility dress had come into general use, but camouflage utility caps were not immediately available. By 1981 both camouflage caps and green 'woolly pully' sweaters were part of Marine field dress.

Left: Enlisted man, 3rd Battalion, 3rd Marines, desert battle dress uniform, Northern Saudi Arabia, 17 January 1991. On the first day of the Gulf War, elements of the 3rd Battalion, 3rd Marines, were positioned just south of Saudi-Kuwait border on the north–south coastal highway. This Marine has on standard infantry dress and equipment, including goggles for use against blowing sand and glare. The camouflage netting on the helmet was characteristic of this battalion.

Top right: Radioman, 1st Marine Division, mission-oriented protective posture uniform (MOPP), Saudi Arabia, November 1990. The very real chemical/biological threat led to frequent training in full MOPP dress. The hood to the gas mask could be tied close to the body.

Bottom right: Marines, 1st Marine Division, northern Saudi Arabia, early February 1991. As the weather became progressively colder through January and into February 1991, the cold-weather night desert camouflage parka coat with liner came into widespread use. Scarves of various types were also necessary against blowing sand. (Photograph by Sergeant Jenks, USMC.)

Left: Lieutenant Colonel Jerry Humble, G-3, 1st Marine Division, Kuwait, 26 February 1991. The British chemical protective suit was provided in limited quantities. Standing next to the division command vehicle while coordinating the ground offensive, Colonel Humble has temporarily dispensed with helmet and equipment. (Photograph by Sergeant Jenks, USMC)

Right: Helicopter crewman with Iraqi prisoner, Kuwait, 25 February 1991. Assisting a wounded Iraqi prisoner, this Marine helicopter crewman has on the standard green Nomex fire-resistant flight suit and white flight helmet without camouflage cover.